INFORMATION TECHNOLOGY

From the abacus to the modern computer has been an extraordinary journey. Take that journey with us, and meet some great machines. There is the computer that came as a box of parts that you put together yourself, and Deep Blue, the computer that could beat the world's best chess player – sometimes. There is Colossus, that saved lives in the Second World War, and the mobile phones that have helped police to catch criminals.

And as well as machines there are people in this story too – good people and bad, rich and poor, clever and stupid. There are Internet millionaires who have helped people all over the world – and there are virus writers who have done terrible damage to computers in dozens of countries.

Come and discover the stories behind the phone in your pocket, and the computer on your desk.

T0364627

OXFORD BOOKWORMS LIBRARY
Factfiles

Information Technology

Stage 3 (1000 headwords)

Factfiles Series Editor: Christine Lindop

PAUL A. DAVIES

Information Technology

OXFORD UNIVERSITY PRESS

OXFORD
UNIVERSITY PRESS

Great Clarendon Street, Oxford OX2 6DP

Oxford University Press is a department of the University of Oxford.
It furthers the University's objective of excellence in research, scholarship,
and education by publishing worldwide in

Oxford New York

Auckland Cape Town Dar es Salaam Hong Kong Karachi
Kuala Lumpur Madrid Melbourne Mexico City Nairobi
New Delhi Shanghai Taipei Toronto

With offices in

Argentina Austria Brazil Chile Czech Republic France Greece
Guatemala Hungary Italy Japan Poland Portugal Singapore
South Korea Switzerland Thailand Turkey Ukraine Vietnam

OXFORD and OXFORD ENGLISH are registered trade marks of
Oxford University Press in the UK and in certain other countries

ISBN 978 0 19 423392 7

A complete recording of this Bookworms edition of *Information Technology* is available

Printed in China

This book is printed on paper from certified and well managed sources.

Word count (main text): 9614

For more information on the Oxford Bookworms
Library, visit www.oup.com/elt/bookworms

The publishers would like to thank the following for permission to reproduce images:

Alamy Images pp viii (microchip/Charlie Newham), 3 (abacus/Dennis Cox), 11 (Commodore/Axel
Hess), 17 (Hotmail/curved-light), 45 (PS2 /Helene Rogers), 46 (virus alert/M.Timothy O'Keefe);
CartoonStock Ltd p 52 (computer crime/Richard Jolley); Corbis pp13 (iMac G5/Apple Computer
Inc/Reuters), 32 (telegraph operator/Keystone), 43 (space invaders/Maranello), 48 (email virus/
Serre Antoine/Sygma); Empics Ltd pp 23 (Sergey Brin & Larry Page/Ben Margot/AP Photos), 39
(fisherman/M.Lakshman/AP Photos), 44 (Wii/Aaron Harris/AP Photo), 55 (robots/Katsumi Kasahara/
AP Photos); Getty Images pp 20 (chess/Stan Honda/AFP), 25 (million dollar homepage/John D
McHugh/AFP), 28 (MySpace webpage/Nicholas Kamm/AFP), 30 (Lily Allen/Jo Hale), 33 (text ticket/
Peter Macdiarmid), 35 (mobile phone/Martin Barraud/Riser), 49 (Sven Jaschan/David Hecker/
AFP), 51 (police/Chris Jackson), 56 (female robot/ChinaFotoPress); Kobal Collection p 18 (I, Robot/
Twentieth Century Fox/Digital Domain); Newscast Limited p 24 (Tom Hadfield/Jim Winslet);
PYMCA p 36 (taking photos/Tristan Fewings); Rex Features pp 6 (difference engine/Kevin Harvey),
16 (Bill Gates/Sipa Press), 26 (Kyle MacDonald/David Boily); Science and Society Picture Library pp
4 (calculating machine), 7 (Ada King/Science Museum Pictorial), 8 (code breaking/Bletchley Park
Trust); Science Photo Library pp 9 (Alan Turing/SPL), 35 (early mobile phone/Tony McConnell).

CONTENTS

1   The computer age

In the nineteenth century, machines changed the world. Suddenly, people could travel more easily and contact one another more quickly. Work changed, too, and many people got jobs in factories. It was the start of the Industrial Age – the age of machines and factories.

The second half of the twentieth century saw the start of the Computer Age. At first, computers were very difficult to use, and only a few people understood them. But soon, computers began to appear in offices and then homes. Today, they are everywhere. Some people still say that they have never used a computer, but they probably use computers every day – they just do not realize it. This is because there are computers in so many things: cars, televisions, radios, washing machines . . .

When the first computers were built in the 1940s and 1950s, they were as big as a room. In 1949, the magazine *Popular Mechanics* made a prediction: 'One day,' they said, 'computers will be really small; in fact, they will weigh less than 1.5 tonnes.' Now, computer chips can be smaller than the full stop at the end of this sentence. Over the past fifty or sixty years, computers have changed much more than people thought possible.

2   In the beginning

For thousands of years, humans have needed to count. Families needed to know how many animals, how much food, and how much land they had. This information was important when people wanted to buy and sell things, and also when people died or got married. There were many different ways to count and write down the numbers. The Sumerians had three different ways: they used one for land, one for fruit and vegetables, and one for animals. They could count, but they had no easy way to do calculations.

Around 1900 to 1800 BC, the Babylonians invented a new way to count using place values. This meant that two things decided the size of a number: the digits (the numbers from 0 to 9), and the place where they were put. Today, we still use place values to count. We can write any number using only ten digits: for example, 134 means 1 x 100, 3 x 10, and 4 x 1. Computers also use place values when they do calculations. They only use two digits (0 and 1): for example, 11011 means 1 x 16, 1 x 8, 0 x 4, 1 x 2, and 1 x 1 (=27). Without place values, fast calculations are impossible.

Between 1000 and 500 BC, the Babylonians invented the abacus. It used small stones which they put in lines. Each line of stones showed a different place value. To do calculations they moved stones from one line to another. Later, different kinds of abacuses were made. Some of them were made of wood and used coloured balls. It is also possible that the abacus was first invented in China, but nobody really knows.

Using an abacus

Leibnitz's Step Reckoner

Although an abacus can be very fast, it is not really a machine because it does not do calculations automatically. In the seventeenth century, people began to build calculating machines. In 1642, the French mathematician Blaise Pascal made an Arithmetic Machine. He used it to count money. During the next ten years, Pascal made fifty more machines.

In the 1670s, a German called Leibnitz continued Pascal's work and made a better machine. Leibnitz's machine was called the Step Reckoner. It could do much more difficult calculations than Pascal's Arithmetic Machine. Interestingly, Leibnitz's machine only used two digits (0 and 1) for its calculations – just like modern computers! In fact, calculating machines like Leibnitz's Step Reckoner were used for the next three hundred years, until cheap computers began to appear.

3   The first computers

The word 'computer' used to mean a person, not a machine. In the nineteenth century, builders and technicians needed to know the answers to very difficult calculations in order to do their work. They did not have the time to do these calculations themselves, so they bought books of answers. The people who did the calculations and wrote the books were called computers.

In the 1820s, a British mathematician called Charles Babbage invented a machine that did very difficult calculations automatically. He called his machine a Difference Engine. He began to build his machine, but he did not finish it because he had a better idea. (Babbage never finished anything – he always had a better idea and started working on something new!) In fact, more than a hundred and fifty years later, some technicians from the Science Museum in London built Babbage's Difference Engine. It is still in the museum today. The machine weighs about three tonnes, and it is nearly two metres tall and three metres wide. And it works: in the early 1990s, it did a calculation and gave the right answer – 31 digits long!

Babbage did not finish making the Difference Engine because he started work on a machine called an Analytical Engine. The Analytical Engine could do more: for example, it had a kind of memory. This meant that it was possible to write programs for it, building on each answer and doing more and more difficult calculations. For this reason, the Analytical Engine is often seen as the first real computer.

However, Babbage never finished building this machine either!

A woman called Ada Lovelace worked with Babbage. She was the daughter of Lord Byron, a famous English writer. Most people did not understand Babbage's ideas, but Ada did, because she was an excellent mathematician. She knew that she could do extraordinary calculations with the Analytical Machine, and she wrote a program for it. Although the machine was never built, Ada Lovelace was still the first computer programmer in the world. In 1979, a modern computer programming language was named ADA.

Babbage's ideas were ahead of their time. Slowly, over

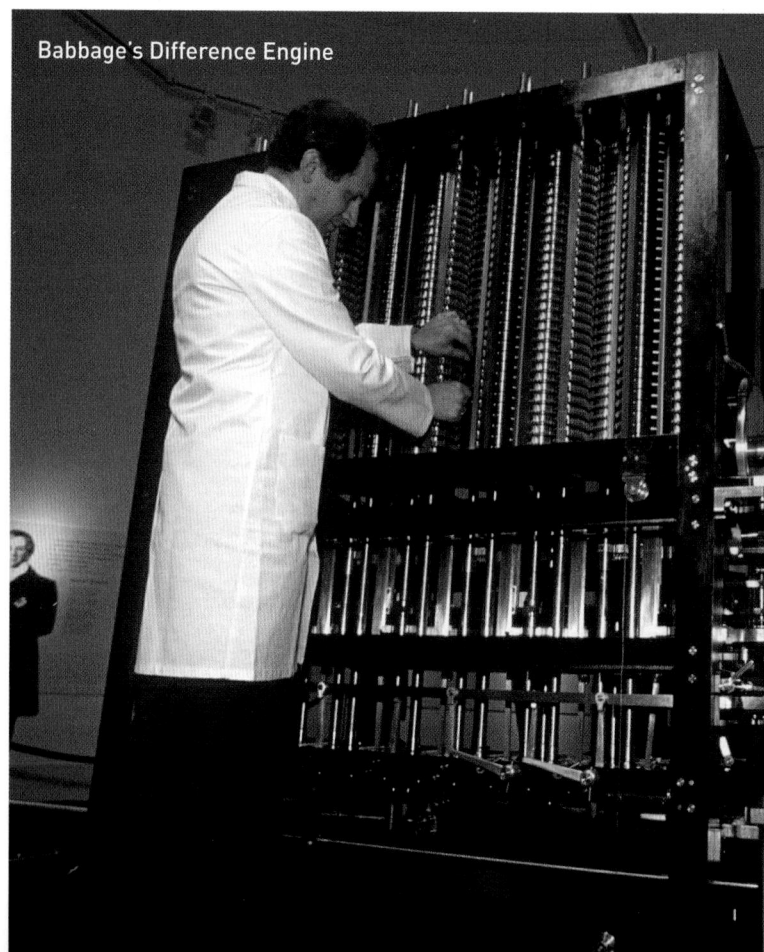

Babbage's Difference Engine

the next one hundred years, inventors began to build better calculating machines. One of the best inventors of the 1930s was a German called Konrad Zuse. In 1938, he built his first machine, the Z1, in his parents' living room in Berlin. His later machines, the Z3 and Z4, were like modern computers in many ways. They used only two digits (0 and 1) to do all the calculations. Also, Zuse wrote programs for his machines by making holes in old cinema film. When he put the film through the machines, they could 'read' the programs and do very long and difficult calculations.

Ada
Lovelace

4 Alan Turing

Alan Turing was born in 1912 in London. He studied mathematics at Cambridge University. In 1937, he wrote a report which talked about a Turing Machine. This was a machine that could read programs and follow any number of instructions. It was only an idea, and he did not have plans to build the machine, but his 1937 report was very important in the history of computing.

In 1939, Turing began to work for the British Government. During the Second World War (1939–1945), the Germans often sent messages from one group of soldiers to another. These messages gave important information and instructions, so of course they were secret. Although the British could get the messages, at first they could not understand them because they were written in a secret code. Turing began working on a computer to break this code.

Turing worked with other mathematicians at a secret place called Bletchley Park. They knew that the Germans were using machines called Enigma machines to send messages in code. To read and understand these messages

Colossus at Bletchley Park, 1943

Alan Turing

you had to have another Enigma machine – and, of course, only the Germans had these.

Turing and the other people at Bletchley built a machine called the Bombe. (Some Polish mathematicians had already built a machine called Bomba to try to break the Enigma code. They worked with the British to build a new and better machine.) By 1942, the workers at Bletchley Park could read and understand all the German messages which used the Enigma code. The film *Enigma*, made in 2001, is about this time at Bletchley Park, and the race to discover the code.

In 1943, the Germans started using a different code. The British called this code Fish. It was much more difficult to understand than the Enigma code. The Bombe machine could not break this code, so the workers at Bletchley Park needed a new computer. In one year, they built Colossus. This was one of the world's first electronic computers which could read and understand programs.

Colossus got its name because of its size: it was as big as a room. It was able to understand difficult codes because it could do thousands of calculations every second. Without Colossus, it took three people six weeks to understand a message written in the Fish code; using Colossus, the British needed only two hours to understand it. A modern PC cannot do the same work any faster.

5 The history of the PC

In 1957, IBM made a computer called the 610 Auto-Point. They said that it was the 'first personal computer'. But it was not like the computers that millions of people have in their homes today. It was large and expensive (55,000 dollars). It was called a personal computer, or PC, because it only

An early PC

needed one person to work it. The first real PCs were not made until seventeen years later.

The first computers (like Colossus) were too big, heavy and expensive to have in your home. But in the 1960s, technicians found a way to make computer chips with thousands of very small transistors on them. In 1971, Intel made a computer chip called the 4004, which had 2,250 transistors. Three years later, they made the 8080, a better and faster chip with 5,000 transistors. An American inventor called Ed Roberts used the Intel 8080 chip to make one of the first PCs. He called his PC the Altair 8800. (The name comes from the television programme *Star Trek*.) When you bought an Altair 8800, you got a box of parts that you put together at home to make your PC. It cost less than 400 dollars, and Ed Roberts sold 2,000 in the first year. The personal computer was on its way.

In 1976, Steve Wozniak and Steve Jobs started the Apple Computer Company. In 1977, their second computer, the Apple 2, appeared. It was popular, and the company made 700,000 dollars that year. The next year, the company made 7 million dollars! Personal computers were here to stay. IBM made their first home computer in 1981. And the *Time* magazine 'person of the year' for 1982 was not a person at all – it was the PC.

In the 1980s, the market for home computers grew very quickly. There were many different computer companies, and each company used its own operating system. The C64, made by Commodore Computers, was the most successful – and in fact, the C64 is still the best-selling home computer in history. Other successful companies were Atari, Amiga, Amstrad, and Acorn. Some companies, like Dell and Compaq, did not use their own operating systems; they

Apple's iMac

made 'IBM compatible' computers. This meant that they used the same operating system and the same software as an IBM PC. IBM compatible computers were more successful than the other kinds of PC, and today nearly all PCs are IBM compatible.

Apple is the only famous computer company which still uses its own operating system. In 1998, it started selling the iMac, a computer that looked very different from other PCs at that time. People chose the iMac because they thought it looked good in their homes. Since 1998, the company has made other new computers that have changed people's ideas about PCs.

Since Intel made the 4004 chip in 1971 with 2,250 transistors, computer chips have become much faster. In fact, the computer technician Gordon Moore made this prediction in 1965: 'The number of transistors on computer chips will double every eighteen months.' This prediction is often called 'Moore's Law' and it seems to be almost true.

Moore's Law and Intel chips

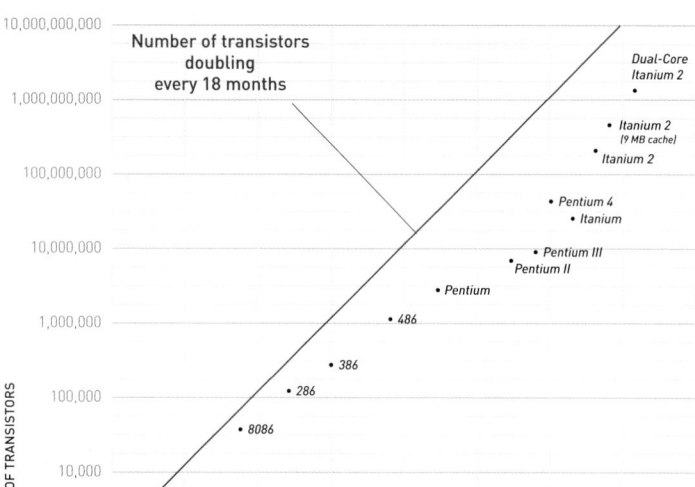

The Intel Pentium 4 chip, made in the year 2000, had 42 million transistors. Two years later, the first Intel Itanium 2 chip had 220 million, and the latest Itanium 2 chips have more than a billion!

As computer chips became smaller and faster during the 1980s, companies began to make laptops – small computers that you could carry around with you. These were very popular with business people because, when they travelled, they could take information with them. With a laptop, they could work at home, in hotel rooms and on aeroplanes.

Because today's computer chips are so fast, modern PCs can do wonderful things. They can copy and keep music, films, and a lot of information, and they can even understand spoken language. A modern laptop is much faster than the very large and expensive computers from the 1970s.

6 Bill Gates and Microsoft

PCs are a very important part of life today, but in the 1970s most people did not know very much about them. One of the first people to see the future of the PC was Bill Gates; because of this, he is now one of the richest people in the world.

Bill Gates was born in Seattle, USA, in 1955. He began to study computer programming at school, when he was thirteen. Later, he went to Harvard University. While he was a student there, he and a friend, Paul Allen, wrote a computer program for the new personal computer, the Altair 8800. They showed it to Ed Roberts, the man who had invented this machine. Ed Roberts liked the software and agreed to use it. Gates and Allen left university early and started their own company – Microsoft.

Microsoft's first big success came in 1981. Apple computers were already very popular, and so the computer company IBM decided to start building PCs. They asked Bill Gates to write an operating system for their PCs, and he wrote MS-DOS. It was not very easy to use, but it was still a big success.

In 1984, Apple made a new computer called a Macintosh. Bill Gates and Microsoft helped to write the operating system for this computer. It was much easier to use than MS-DOS because there were pictures that showed you what to do instead of difficult instructions. Later, Microsoft made

their own operating system which used pictures – they called it Windows. Windows became the most successful piece of software in the history of computing. By 1986, Bill Gates was already a billionaire at the age of thirty-one.

In the 1990s, Microsoft became even larger. In 1995, the new operating system (Windows 95) came with a piece of software that let people use the Internet. Soon, millions of people were paying Microsoft twenty dollars a month to use the Internet.

Most personal computers use the Windows operating system, so people usually buy Microsoft software too. It is difficult for small software companies to show their programs to people. Many people are unhappy about Microsoft because they think the company is too big and powerful. In 2001, judges in the USA said that Microsoft had to share information about its operating system and software with other companies.

Since the 1990s, the Internet has given people a chance to find out about other kinds of software. Some programmers do not want money for their software – they just want to share ideas with other computer programmers. They call this kind of software 'shareware'. However, a lot of people are happy to pay money for the software which they use at home and in the office, so the future of Microsoft and other software companies is probably safe.

Bill Gates has been one of the richest people in the world for about twenty years. In 2000, he and his wife started

Bill Gates

the Bill and Melinda Gates Foundation, and they have already given it more than twenty-eight billion dollars. The Foundation helps the poorest people in the USA and around the world. It pays for work to fight against diseases like malaria and AIDS. It also helps schools and other places where people go to learn. In May 2005, it gave 11 million dollars to schools and colleges in Chicago, and since 2000, it has given 250 million dollars to libraries across the USA for new computers.

Microsoft's Internet service, MSN

7 Humans against computers

For more than a hundred years, writers have been interested in the power of machines – and what happens when they go wrong. Before computers became part of modern life, they began to appear in stories. Often, these computers begin working for humans, but later they refuse to do this and start to do frightening and dangerous things.

A good example of this kind of story is *I Have No Mouth And I Must Scream*, by Harlan Ellison, published in 1967. Three very large and powerful countries use computers to

Will Smith, in *I, Robot*

fight against one another, but the computers become angry with the humans. They work together to kill all the humans in the world except for five people, who the computers keep like animals. Later, films like *2001: A Space Odyssey* and *I, Robot* used stories of this kind too.

The idea of computers that are more powerful than humans is interesting to scientists too. That is why IBM spent a lot of time and money building a chess computer called Deep Blue. They wanted to show that a computer could win against Gary Kasparov, the best chess player in the world.

In 1996, Deep Blue played Kasparov six times. Kasparov won the match, but IBM knew that their computer could do better. They did a lot of work on the computer and its software, and in 1997, Deep Blue and Kasparov played again. This time, Deep Blue won the match (3.5 to 2.5).

A lot of newspapers wrote about Deep Blue and Kasparov.

Kasparov plays Deep Blue

They said that it was the beginning of a new age: computers had finally become more intelligent than humans. However, Deep Blue had help from humans. Its software was written by five different computer technicians and a very good chess player. Also, it is important to remember that chess is a mathematical game. Computers are good at chess because they can do millions of calculations every second. Deep Blue can look at 200,000,000 different chess moves every second; a human chess player like Kasparov can look at three! In some ways, it is surprising that computers do not win at chess every time. In 2003, Kasparov played against a new chess computer, Deep Junior, and the match ended 3–3.

Computers can follow instructions and play mathematical games very well, but are they really intelligent? Do they really think in the same way that humans think? These are difficult questions, and scientists do not always agree on the answers. Some scientists believe that the human brain is just like a very powerful computer; so if we can make a computer that is powerful enough, it will think like a human brain.

Other scientists believe that the human brain does not do calculations in the same way as a computer. They think that perhaps one day a really powerful computer will do some of the things that a human brain does, but it will never really think like one.

In the past, people thought that computers did not have any imagination – they could never invent funny stories, or write beautiful music. However, software programmers have recently 'taught' computers to do many different things which need imagination. For example, Paul Hodgson is a programmer and his favourite music is jazz. He wrote some music software for his computer, and now the computer can invent pieces of music in the same way as a jazz musician. The computer is not a very good jazz musician – but as the software gets better, so will the music.

In fact, music, like chess, is quite mathematical. Perhaps it is not a surprise that computers are good at both. One of the first computer technicians, Alan Turing, was interested in the question 'Can a computer really think like a human?', so he invented the Turing Test. To do the test, you sit at a computer and 'talk' (using messages) to someone in a different room. That 'someone' can be a person or a computer, but you do not know which it is. If you think it is a person but it is really a computer, then that computer has passed the Turing Test.

Every year programmers try to write software which makes their computer pass the Turing Test. There is a prize of 100,000 dollars – the Loebner Prize – for the first computer to pass the test. Alan Turing himself made this prediction: 'A computer will pass the Turing Test before the end of the twentieth century.' But he was wrong, and so far, nobody has won the prize.

8 The Internet

The Internet began in the 1970s as a way to send information from one computer to another. It was only used by people who worked in governments and universities. But in the 1990s, it suddenly began to be more popular.

In the early 1990s, a British man called Tim Berners-Lee invented the 'Web'. With the Web it was much easier to find information on the Internet, and to move from one part of the Internet to another. By the end of the 1990s, millions of people around the world were using the Web for many different things: for example, working, shopping, playing games, and studying.

In the first half of the 1990s, it was clear that the Internet and the Web were changing the world for ever. Hundreds of new companies started on the Internet. They knew that the Internet was growing, and that it offered an easy way to do business with millions of people. The banks were very happy to give money to these new 'Internet start-up' companies because they seemed to be the future. However, by the end of the 1990s there were too many of these companies. They could not all be successful, and many of them went out of business. Now, only the best of the Internet start-up companies are making money.

Although most Internet start-up companies are not successful, a few of them have become some of the biggest companies in the world. In 1996, two students at Stanford University, California, invented a new and better kind of search engine – a program that helps people to find information on the Web. Their names were Larry Page and Sergey Brin, and they called their search engine 'Google'. They started a company in 1997, with an office in a friend's garage! The company grew very quickly, and today has nearly 6,000 people working for it. The Google search engine does about 1 billion searches every day for users around the world, and the 450,000 computers at the company's offices remember them all! Larry Page and Sergey Brin are now two of the richest people in the world.

Pierre Omidyar is another Internet billionaire. Omidyar worked for a software company as a computer programmer, and in 1995, he started a website where people could buy and sell almost anything. He called it 'Auction Web' but soon changed the name to 'eBay'. At first, the website was something that Omidyar did in his own time, but the number of people who used it grew quickly and eBay became a successful company. Today, more than 180 million people use the website, and almost everything you can think of has been sold, from some water in a cup used by Elvis

Google inventors
Sergey Brin and Larry Page

Tom Hadfield

Presley (for 455 dollars) to a town (Bridgeville, California, for nearly 2 million dollars).

Young people often know more about computing and the Internet than older people. For this reason, some very young people have had a lot of success with Internet start-up companies. Tom Hadfield began using computers at the age of two. When he was twelve, he began putting football scores on the Internet, just because he liked football. This soon became a business called Soccernet. During the 1998 World Cup, 300,000 people visited the Soccernet website every day. In 1999, Tom and his father sold 60 per cent of Soccernet to Disney for 15 million pounds. Tom and his father also started another Internet company called Schoolsnet, which has information for students and teachers. Thanks to the Internet, Tom Hadfield became a very successful businessman before he left school!

One good idea can be enough to make a lot of money on the Internet. In 2005, Alex Tew, a British teenager, needed money to study at university. He sat down in his bedroom with a piece of paper and a pen and wrote 'How can I become a millionaire?' Twenty minutes later, he thought of the 'Million Dollar Homepage'. The idea was to let companies advertise on his website for one dollar a pixel. (Pixels are the tiny dots that make the pictures you see on your computer.) Soon news of his website was on television and in the newspapers, and a lot of companies bought pixels on his website. When he had sold 999,000 pixels for 999,000 dollars, he decided to sell the final 1,000 pixels on eBay. Instead of 1,000 dollars, he got more than 38,000 dollars for them!

Canadian Kyle MacDonald had a more unusual idea. He wanted a house but did not have enough money to buy one.

So he decided to trade things on the Internet. He started with a red paperclip and traded it for a pen. Then he traded the pen for something else. He continued trading and, exactly a year later, he got a house!

Today, almost every company in the world has got a website on the Internet. Each website has got a web address – its own special name which you use to visit the site. In the early 1990s, before most companies had really thought about the Internet, some people got web addresses with the names of famous companies – for example, Panasonic and Hertz. These people were not part of the companies; they were hoping to sell the web addresses to the companies for a lot of money one day in the future. This was called 'cyber-squatting'. Since 1999, new international laws have made cyber-squatting impossible.

Kyle MacDonald and the red paperclip

9   **Power to the people**

The Internet is changing the way that people live. Things are possible now that people could not even think of twenty or thirty years ago. It is often difficult to control what happens on the Internet, because people can use it from anywhere in the world. In January 1999, an American University student called Shawn Fanning invented a piece of software that could copy music. In May of the same year, he started a company called Napster. Internet users could visit Napster and use its software to copy their favourite music. Suddenly, they did not need to buy CDs. Of course, the music companies were not very happy about this. A lot of musicians were also unhappy, because people could get their music for free. In the end, Napster agreed to pay money to the music companies and musicians. But it is still easy for Internet users to get free music – and films too – by using file-sharing software. With this software, users can share information on their computer (songs, pictures, films, etc) with any other computer in the world that has the same software. Music companies are trying to stop this, of course. In 2005, ninety people in the UK had to pay about 2,500 pounds each because they had put thousands of songs on their computers for other people to copy. In the USA, more than 18,000 people have had to pay for file-sharing. But millions of Internet users go on file-sharing every day, and it will become more and more difficult to stop it.

At its best, the Internet is a great way for people all over the world to share their information and ideas. Before the

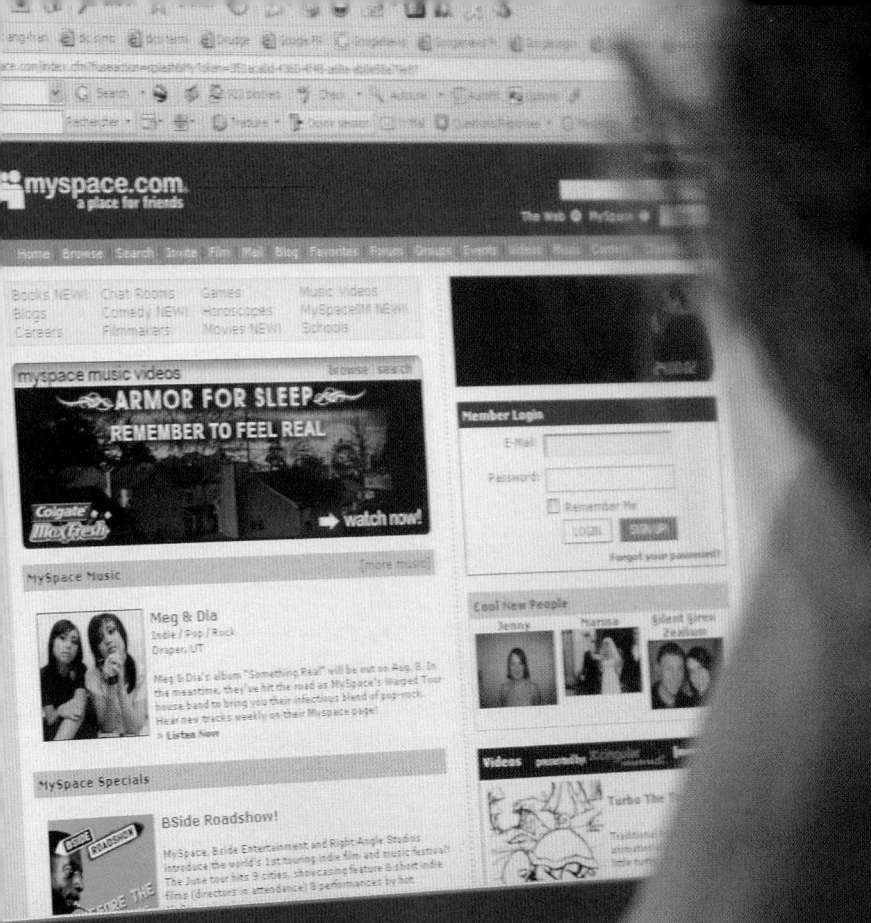

Internet, information about the world came from places like newspapers, TV programmes, and books. The companies that made the newspapers, books, and programmes controlled the information that people could get. Of course, those companies are still very powerful, but the Internet is getting more and more powerful, and nobody controls it. People can find information for themselves from places all over the world.

In the past, you could not write and sell a book until you found a company that liked your ideas and agreed to help you. This is because it cost a lot of money to make the books. But today, Internet bookshops like Amazon sell thousands of different books that are 'printed on demand'

– they make the books one by one, when somebody visits the website and wants to buy one.

The same is true for music. If you are a band and want to make and sell music, you do not need a music company. You can put the music on your own website and people can pay to copy it. This saves money and time – you do not need to make CDs or ask shops to sell them. And your customers can be anywhere in the world.

Millions of people around the world use the Internet to give information about themselves, and to read about other people and make friends. They do this on websites like MySpace. MySpace is one of the most popular websites in the world; on 9 August 2006, it had exactly 100 million users, and it gets about 500,000 new users every week. Each user has their own pages on the website, where they can put photos, music, videos, and information. They also have a 'blog' (or 'web log'), which is like a diary where they say what they have done and how they are feeling. British singer Lily Allen put her songs onto her MySpace page in November 2005. Thousands of people listened to them and talked about them. In July 2006 her song *Smile* was number one in Britain, but many people had heard it weeks or months before.

Most information on the Internet is free – and you can find information about almost everything. For many people the first place to look is the Wikipedia website. This began in 2001, and by 2007 it had information on more than 6 million subjects in more than 200 different languages. Anyone can use it, and anyone can add more information to the website.

The Internet is still young and it is still growing fast. It has already changed our world in a lot of different ways, and the changes will continue. At the moment, it is not easy for people in the poorest countries of the world to use the Internet, but this is changing too. Although the Internet can make problems in some ways, it can also bring people around the world closer together, and make them more powerful.

Lily Allen

10 Getting the message

Although the first e-mail message was sent in 1971, electronic messages began nearly two hundred years earlier. The first telegraph machine was built in 1774. These machines sent messages along wires from one place to another. But for the next sixty years, the machines were very large and difficult to use, and each one needed twenty-six wires – one for each letter of the alphabet. In the 1840s, an American inventor called Samuel Morse built a better kind of telegraph which only needed one wire. He also invented a special code for messages – Morse code. Immediately, telegraphs became an important way for people to send information. During the next twelve years, American telegraph companies put up 58,000 kilometres of telegraph wires to send messages all over the USA.

In the 1920s, a new kind of electronic message was invented – the telex. A telex machine could send a message to any other telex machine in the world. They did not use telephone or telegraph wires – they used telex lines. These lines were quite expensive, and the machines were not easy to use, but the system worked. Companies continued to use telex until the 1980s and many companies still have telex machines today.

In the 1980s, people began to buy personal computers. Soon, it was possible to send e-mail messages from one PC to another, but both people had to be part of the same e-mail system. There were several different e-mail systems, and it was not possible to send messages from one system

Sending a telegraph

to another. For this reason, e-mails did not immediately become popular.

In the 1990s, people began to use the Internet and the Web. This made it easier to send e-mail messages because there was only one system. E-mails soon became a very popular (and very cheap) way to send messages to anywhere in the world. In the late 1990s, people started to send another kind of electronic message: they used their mobile phones to send text messages. Now they could send or receive messages in any place and at any time.

At the beginning of the twenty-first century, millions of people started to use Instant Messaging software: 'Yahoo Messenger' and AOL's 'Aim' are two of the most popular. Users of this software can send and receive messages instantly: as one person writes their message, the words appear on the other person's computer. You do not even need to be at your computer; you can have the same software on your mobile phone. Getting the message has never been quicker or easier.

11 Mobile phones

The first mobile phone call was made in New York in 1973, but it was ten years before you could buy a mobile phone in a shop. In 1985, you could buy one in the UK for about 2,000 pounds. It was as big as a laptop computer, and it only had enough power for twenty minutes of conversation. Also, with these early phones it was very easy for somebody with another phone to listen to your conversations. But they still became popular with rich young business people.

After about ten years, mobile phones suddenly started to become very popular. The mobile phone company Vodafone needed nine years to get their first million users, but only eighteen months to get their second million. (In 2007 they had 14 million users in the UK alone.) The change happened because people started to use mobile phones not just for business, but to talk to their family and friends. People's idea of a telephone started to change. In the past, a phone number was something that belonged to a place: a house, a restaurant, a business. Now, phones are things that people carry with them, and the number belongs to the person, not the place. Today, it is difficult to talk about the number of users in the world because it is changing so quickly. In 2004, the number passed 1 billion; it passed 2 billion only two years later, in 2006. Some countries – for example, Hong Kong – have more mobile phones than people.

In the late 1990s, people started using their phones to send text messages. In 2000, 17 billion messages were sent in the world; in 2001, 250 billion messages were sent; in 2004, 500 billion. That is 100 messages for every person in the world!

Text messages use their own kind of language. Long text messages are not easy to send or read, so people find ways to make them shorter. For example, a message in English can say 'RUOK?' (Are you OK?), or 'B4' (before). This way, you

Mobile phones,
then and now

Taking photos with mobile phones

can send a message in just a few letters and numbers: for example, 'CU L8R 4 T'. ('See you later for tea.') Speakers of other languages do the same thing. For example, in Mandarin Chinese, you can send the numbers '520' (*wu er ling*) which sound like the words for 'I love you' (*wo ai ni*).

James Trusler from Sussex in England is one of the world's fastest texters. James sends a lot of text messages – about 2,500 a month. Luckily, he works for Vodafone, so he does not have to pay for them. In 2003 he appeared on an Australian TV programme and texted this message in 67 seconds: 'The razor-toothed piranhas of the genera Serrasalmus and Pygocentrus are the most ferocious freshwater fish in the world. In reality they seldom attack a human.' It was the fastest time in the world. (Try it yourself!) But three years later, Ang Chuang Yang, a 16-year-old student from Singapore, sent the same message – in 41.5 seconds!

Today, you can make calls and send texts, but you can do a lot of other things with mobile phones too. Nearly all phones now have a camera, and you can take pictures, listen to music, play computer games, and go on the Internet. And modern phones look very different from the large, heavy mobile phones that appeared in the 1980s. Today's phones are small and beautiful – and for many people, it's important to have the newest and best phone.

A fisherman calls the market

Mobile phones have changed the lives of people all over the world. In the past, you could only phone friends and family when they were at home, but now they can be in any place when you speak to them. Many people who travel alone feel safer with a mobile phone.

People in poorer countries are also using mobile phones to make their lives better. For example, in Bangladesh, farmers pay for a few mobile phone calls to find the best prices before they take their food to market. This way, they get more money for their food, and the owner of the phone gets a little money for each call too. Nearly half the people in Bangladesh live on less than one dollar a day, but more and more of them are using mobile phones.

Sometimes, a mobile phone can save your life. In 2005, a British scientist called John Gillatt was staying at a hotel in Malaysia and decided to go for a short walk in the jungle, where he got lost. For two days, he tried to get back to the hotel, but he couldn't get out of the jungle. In the end, he

phoned his wife in England. She contacted his hotel and they called the police. They started to search for Mr Gillatt, but it took another three days to find him. During that time, he stayed in contact with the searchers and his family by phone. When the searchers found him, he was tired, hungry, and thirsty, but alive. He believes that the text messages of love from his family in England helped him to stay alive.

Making calls is not the only way a phone can help you at a difficult time. Five students from Newcastle University in the UK were climbing a mountain when the weather became very bad and they could not get down from the mountain. Night came, and the students were cold, wet, and frightened. They used a mobile phone to call for help. When searchers arrived at the mountain, they could not find the students because it was too dark. Then one of the students accidentally took a photo with his phone. The searchers saw the light from the phone and asked the students to take more photos. Then they climbed towards the light and found the students.

Mobile phones can also help the police to fight crime. Every time somebody makes a call on a mobile phone, the phone company keeps information about the time and place of the call. The police can sometimes get this information about calls from the phone companies if it helps them with a serious crime. More and more often, this information is an important part of police work because it shows where somebody was at a certain time and who they spoke to. And because mobile phones have cameras, it is easy for people to take photos if they see a crime and then send the photos to the police.

There are other ways that mobile phones can help the police. In April 2005, police in Rogersville, Tennessee, in the USA caught two men stealing things from a house. One of the men had a mobile phone in his pocket, and he knocked the buttons which called 911, the number for the police. The two men did not know that the police were listening to their conversation! Another time, a different thief dropped his mobile phone while he was stealing things from a house. The police found the phone and used the information in the phone to find its owner – the thief! Other criminals have helped police because they used their phones to take photos of their own crimes.

But mobile phones make problems too. Because they are

small, and people always carry them in their bags or pockets, they are easy for criminals to steal. Children are becoming victims of crime more often than in the past because they carry mobile phones.

Some people are worried that phones are bad for people's health, and they are unhappy that more and more young children are using them. Mobile phones also make the roads more dangerous, because people use them while they are driving (although this is a crime in many countries).

Some people have problems because they cannot stop using their mobile phones. In 2005, a teenager from the UK needed help because he could not stop sending text messages. He was sending about 700 messages a week, and spending 4,500 pounds a year on them. Scientists believe that this problem is growing quickly among young people.

Although there are many problems with mobile phones, the number of users continues to grow. By 2015, there will probably be 4 billion. And people are using their phones for more and more different things: watching TV and videos, instant messaging, and shopping on the Internet. It seems that nothing can stop the mobile phone.

12 Computer games

In the early 1960s, the computer company DEC made a computer called PDP-1. PDP-1s were large and expensive (120,000 dollars), so only companies and universities bought them. Steve Russell, a student at one of these universities, wrote a piece of software for the PDP-1. It was a game for two players, and he called it *Spacewar*. The two players controlled spaceships which fought against each other. Users of the PDP-1 liked the game, and other programmers made the software better.

In the late 1960s, a programmer called Donald Woods invented a game called *Adventure*. This was a different kind of game from *Spacewar* because it did not have any pictures and it was for one player only. The computer told a story; the player became part of the story, and gave the computer instructions, like 'Go south', or 'Get the box'.

Together, *Spacewar* and *Adventure* started the two most important kinds of computer games: games with fast action, and games with stories and imagination. But it was a few years before computer games became popular. In 1971, a student called Nolan Bushnell tried to make money from the game *Spacewar*. People did not have PCs then, so he built a machine for bars, shopping centres, and other places where people meet. To play the game, people had to put money in the machine. A company bought Nolan Bushnell's idea for 500 dollars and made 1,500 machines. But nobody wanted to play the game.

Nolan Bushnell decided that the space game was too difficult. He used his 500 dollars to start his own company,

An early computer game

Atari, and invented a much easier game. It was a tennis game called *Pong*, and it was very easy to play. People loved it! In 1976, Bushnell sold Atari for 28 million dollars. Computer games were here to stay.

Since the 1980s, computer games have changed a lot. Computers are much more powerful now, so the games are much faster and use fantastic pictures. The biggest companies in computer games today are Sony (who make PlayStation), Nintendo (who make Wii), and Microsoft (who make Xbox). With some games, the computer can 'feel' when the player moves. And two or more players can use the Internet to play together when they are in different parts of the world.

How much better can games become? If you have seen *Star Trek: The Next Generation* on television, perhaps you have seen the games room on the spaceship. People can play games with extraordinary stories which look and feel real. This kind of game is still in the future, but perhaps not very far in the future.

Millions of people around the world enjoy playing computer games. They spend more than 20 billion dollars

a year on them. They are a lot of fun – but some people are worried that they also make problems.

Many computer games are violent: they have a lot of guns and fighting. Some people believe that playing these games can make young people more violent in real life. In 2004, a British teenager killed a 14-year-old schoolboy. Before the crime, the killer had spent hours playing a violent computer game called *Manhunt*. After the crime, shops around the UK stopped selling *Manhunt*. But many people do not agree that computer games make young people more violent or change what they do.

Most people agree that it is not good for your health to spend hours and hours playing computer games. In August 2005, a South Korean man died after playing a computer

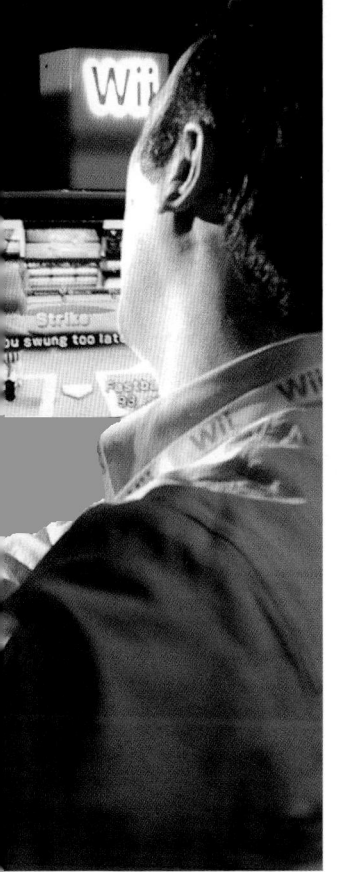

game for forty-nine hours without food or sleep. This is, of course, very unusual. But there are large numbers of young people who prefer playing computer games to walking, cycling, or playing sport. Many of these young people are getting fatter and less healthy because they are not active enough. It is a serious problem in many countries, and it is getting worse. Perhaps in the future people will find a way to make playing computer games a lot more active.

13

I love you (and other viruses)

A virus is a kind of computer program. It moves from one computer to another and damages the computer's memory or other parts of the machine. Some viruses are difficult to stop; they can damage millions of computers in a very short time.

The first virus appeared in 1986. It was called Brain. In 1987, a more dangerous virus called Jerusalem appeared. This virus stayed in a computer and did nothing until the date was Friday the thirteenth; then it started to damage the computer's memory. Soon programmers began to write anti-virus software. Each new virus was more difficult to find, and so anti-virus software needed to get better and better. By 1988, newspapers and magazines were beginning to have stories about viruses.

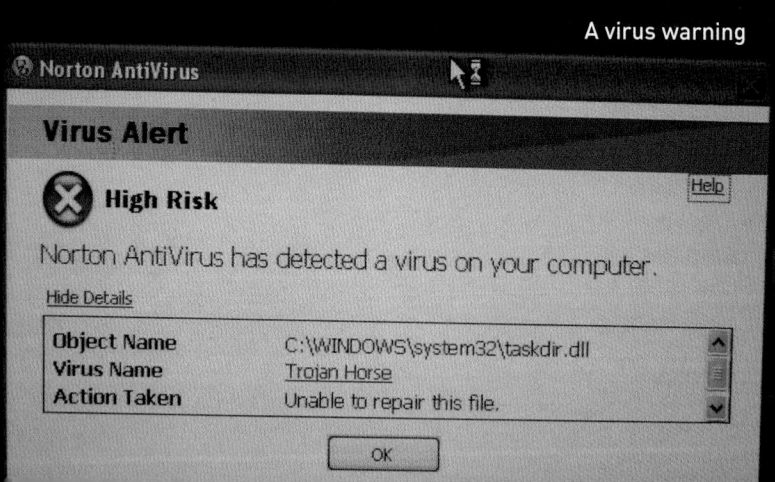

A virus warning

By the early 1990s, there were more than 150 computer viruses in the world. Some of these viruses were more 'intelligent' than others: they had special software which made it very difficult for people to fight the virus. One programmer who wrote a few different viruses around this time is known as the Dark Avenger. He (or she) probably lives in Bulgaria, but the police have never found them. In 1993, the SatanBug virus appeared in Washington DC. The anti-virus software companies worked with the police to find the programmer, who was just a teenager.

By the late 1990s, most computers were part of the e-mail and Internet systems. This meant that virus programmers could do a lot of damage very quickly. For example, in 1999, the Melissa virus appeared. It could move from one computer to another by e-mail. A year later, the most successful virus in history reached millions of computers in less than twenty-four hours. When it appeared on a computer, it automatically sent itself to every other e-mail address in the computer. This virus was called I Love You. The person who made the virus was probably a very clever 23-year-old computer student from the Philippines called Onel de Guzman. He has never said that he wrote it, but detectives know that the virus came from his computer. Onel de Guzman was not punished for his crime because in May 2000 the Philippines did not have any laws against computer crime (although they do now!)

Onel de Guzman is not the only young computer programmer who became famous because of a virus. In 2004, on the evening of his eighteenth birthday, a teenager from a small town in Germany sent a message from his computer. Within three hours, the computers in hospitals and banks in Hong Kong had stopped working, planes in the USA could not fly, and trains in Australia and the USA had stopped.

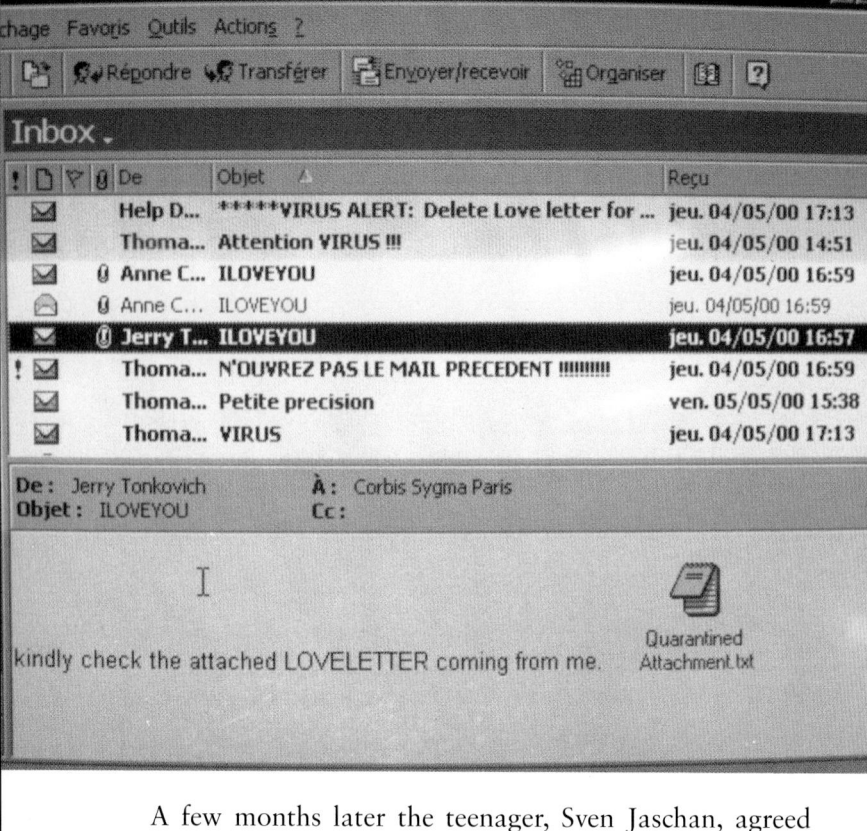

A few months later the teenager, Sven Jaschan, agreed that he had written the Sasser computer virus and put it on the Internet. He did not go to prison because he was only seventeen – and so not an adult – when he wrote the virus program.

Sven had spent a lot of time writing the Sasser virus on the computer in his bedroom. He often spent ten hours a day in front of his computer but his parents had not known what he was doing at the time. When he put the virus on the Internet, he did not realise it would cause so many problems – he was just very happy that it had worked. 'I told my friends at school,' he said, 'and they thought it was great.' But one of his classmates contacted Microsoft and told the company about him. Microsoft had offered 250,000 dollars for information about the virus.

The virus programmers are getting better all the time,

but so is the anti-virus software. In fact, virus programmers often go to work for computer companies, because they know how to make computers safe. Some people think that viruses will do a lot more damage in the future. Computers are now an important part of everything; without them, the modern world would stop. Nobody would be able to travel, work, shop, watch television, get money, or send messages. Perhaps one day, a computer virus will bring the world to a stop for a few hours.

Virus maker Sven Jaschan

14   Computer crime

In 2001, police in New York arrested Abraham Abdallah. Mr Abdallah worked in a restaurant kitchen, where his job was to wash dishes. But when he was not at work, he pretended to be some of the richest and most famous people in the world – people like Steven Spielberg, Ted Turner, and Oprah Winfrey. Using the Internet, he got information about his victims – their addresses, the numbers of their bank accounts and so on. He then pretended to be these people and took money from their accounts. This kind of crime is called identity theft, and it is happening more often. Mr Abdallah stole about 80 million dollars before the police caught him.

You do not have to be rich or famous to be the victim of identity theft. In fact, about one person in ten in the UK believes that it has happened to them. There are lots of different ways for criminals to find the information that they need. They can get it from your old computer, or from old letters that they find in your rubbish. Or they can use software to take the information from your computer while you are using the Internet. Often, people are victims of identity theft and never know it.

People use phishing (pronounced the same as 'fishing') to try to get information from their victims. An e-mail arrives that pretends to be from a large, well-known company: for example, a bank, or eBay. The e-mail asks the victim to go to a company website and put in their name, account number, and other information about themselves. But the website does not in fact belong to the company – it belongs

Police removing computers used in crime

to criminals. If the victim follows the instructions, the criminals then have the information that they need to get money from the victim's bank account.

In 2005, police in London stopped criminals stealing 220 million pounds from the London offices of the Japanese bank Sumitomo Mitsui. The criminals used the Internet to put special software on the bank's computers. This software remembers all the letters and numbers that are put into the computer. The criminals planned to use this information to get money from bank accounts. They were not successful, but they showed people that it was possible. Banks spend millions of dollars a year trying to stop new kinds of computer crime.

Some kinds of computer crime are not new – people have known about them for many years, sometimes hundreds of years. But with the Internet, criminals can find more victims more quickly and in more places, even across the world. One of the oldest kinds of crime, the 'Spanish Prisoner', began in the sixteenth century. It works like this. The criminal tells his victim that a very rich and important person is in prison in Spain. If the victim gives some money to help get the important person out of prison, he will receive a lot more money in the future. But he must tell nobody about this. Of course, there is no prisoner; it is all a lie. When the criminal has got as much money from the victim as possible, he disappears. These days, criminals use e-mail to contact thousands of people all over the world as they look for victims. Usually the criminal pretends to have lots of money – thousands or millions of dollars – that he needs to move out of banks in Africa. He asks the victim for money to help him do this, and promises to give the victim a lot more money in the future. Although this kind of crime is well known (it is sometimes called 'Nigerian letter' or '419') the criminals still find new victims. In fact, this crime is big business and may involve about 250,000 people. They often send their e-mails from Internet cafés, not from their own computers. Then when the police look for the criminals, they cannot find them.

There are new kinds of crime now because of shopping on the Internet. These are usually very simple: you promise to sell something, take the money, and then you do not send it to the buyer. A teenager from Wales, Philip Shortman, did this for thirteen months with more than 100 eBay customers. He made more than 45,000 pounds and spent it on holidays, clothes, mobile phones and TVs. He had to give back 615 pounds – the only money he had left – and also had to spend a year in prison.

15   The future

'I think there is a world market for maybe five computers.' This prediction was made in 1943 by T. J. Watson, the head of IBM. Today, there are hundreds of millions of PCs in homes all around the world. It is not easy to make predictions about computers! You can only look at the recent past and try to see where we are going in the future.

Since the first computers were built in the 1940s, they have become smaller and more powerful every few years. Will computers get smaller and smaller in the future? Probably not – for two reasons. Firstly, by the year 2020 the transistors on computer chips will be as small as possible. Secondly, a very small personal computer is difficult to use (and easy to lose). At the moment, it is possible to build a computer which you can put in your pocket, or wear like a watch. Perhaps this is as small as we need.

A lot of computer scientists are working on Artificial Intelligence. This is software which makes computers think more like humans. There are still many things which are very easy for humans but very difficult for computers: for example, understanding language. Some computers can understand words when a person speaks, but they cannot really have a conversation – they can only follow instructions. However, this kind of software is getting better every year. Soon, we will probably be able to talk to a computer in the same way that we talk to a friend.

Robots at work in the home

Computer scientists are also trying to build computers which can see. It is easy to make a computer with 'eyes', but very difficult for the computer to understand what it sees. Most people think that computers will do many different jobs in the world of the future – perhaps they will drive taxis or work in shops. But to do these jobs, they will need to see and understand the world around them. In August 2006, Miss Rong Cheng started work in a science museum in China. She can speak and understand Mandarin. Miss Rong Cheng is a robot, and she was built by a group of Chinese scientists. At the moment, computers like Miss Rong Cheng cannot do any job as well as a human, but perhaps that will change in the future.

Moore's Law says that the number of transistors on

Miss Rong Cheng

computer chips doubles every eighteen months. This has been true for the past thirty years, but by about 2020 we will have the smallest transistors possible. Then a new kind of computer will be necessary. At the moment, scientists are building the first quantum computers. In the future, these will be much faster and more powerful than any computer that we have now. Or perhaps a different kind of computer will appear before then. That is why it is difficult to make predictions about the future of computing: the future is often closer than you think it is.

GLOSSARY

account an agreement that you have with a bank to keep your money there

action fast exciting events

advertise to tell people about something you want to sell

brain the part of the head that thinks and remembers

calculation using numbers to find out an amount

code words or numbers that hold a secret message

contact *(v & n)* to speak or write to somebody

control to have power over something or somebody

copy to make something that is the same as something else

double to become twice as many

electronic using electricity

government a group of people who control a country

head the most important person in an organization

history things that happened in the past

human of people (not animals or machines)

imagination making pictures in your mind

instructions information about how to do something

invent to make something that did not exist before; *(n)* **invention**

judge the person in court who decides how to punish somebody

jungle a place with thick forest in a hot country

law (1) one of the rules of a country; (2) a rule that explains what happens in a certain situation

mathematician a person whose job is working with numbers

memory the part of a brain or of a machine that remembers things

museum a place where you can look at old or interesting things

musician a person who plays music as a job

operating system the software that lets computers understand programs

paperclip a small piece of wire that holds papers together

power being able to control people or things; *(adj)* **powerful**

prediction saying what you think will happen

program   instructions for a computer to follow

receive   to get something that is sent to you

scientist   a person who studies natural things

score   the number of points that teams get in a game

share   to let other people use something that is yours

software   computer programs

space   the place beyond earth where the moon and stars are

system   a group of things that work together

technician   a person who works with machines

teenager   a person who is between thirteen and nineteen years old

telegraph   an old machine for sending messages

text *(v & n)*   to send a written message using a mobile phone

trade   to change something that you have for something that somebody else has

transistor   an electronic switch

victim   someone who suffers as the result of a crime

war   fighting between armies of different countries

website   a place on the Internet where a person or company puts information

wire   a thin piece of metal

Information Technology

ACTIVITIES

ACTIVITIES

Before Reading

1 **Read the back cover of the book, and the introduction on the first page. Are these sentences true (T) or false (F)?**

1 The first computer program was written twenty years ago.
2 Colossus was a computer that helped to save lives.
3 The computer is older than the abacus.
4 Deep Blue is a computer that can write music.
5 A virus can do terrible damage to computers.

2 **Is information technology important in your life? How often do you …**

1 … send e-mails?
2 … look for information on the Internet?
3 … take photos with a mobile phone?
4 … listen to music on an MP3 player?
5 … play computer games?

3 **Read these sentences. For each sentence, circle 1 (strongly disagree), 2 (disagree), 3 (not sure), 4 (agree), or 5 (strongly agree).**

1 Information technology has made people's lives better in a lot of ways. 1 / 2 / 3 / 4 / 5
2 In the future, people won't have to work hard, because computers will do most of the work. 1 / 2 / 3 / 4 / 5
3 People are getting fat and lazy because they spend too much time using computers. 1 / 2 / 3 / 4 / 5
4 Older people don't need to use information technology – it's for young people. 1 / 2 / 3 / 4 / 5

ACTIVITIES

While Reading

Read Chapters 1 and 2. Then complete the sentences with the words and phrases below.

in 1642 / in the 1940s and 1950s / in the nineteenth century / about three thousand years ago / every day

1 The Industrial Age started _____.
2 Many people use computers _____.
3 The first computers were built _____.
4 The abacus was invented _____.
5 A French mathematician made an Arithmetic Machine _____.

Read Chapters 3 and 4, then circle a, b, or c.

1 At first, the word 'computer' meant a _____.
  a) book   b) person   c) machine
2 The machine invented by Charles Babbage in the 1820s weighs about three _____.
  a) grams   b) kilos   c) tonnes
3 Ada Lovelace's father was the _____ Lord Byron.
  a) engineer   b) poet   c) mathematician
4 Ada Lovelace was the first computer _____ in the world.
  a) programmer b) designer   c) builder
5 Konrad Zuse made programs for his machines using _____.
  a) paper   b) glass   c) cinema film
6 Alan Turing built a machine to understand the _____ code.
  a) Enigma   b) Bletchley   c) Bomba
7 The computer Colossus was the size of a _____.
  a) desk   b) room   c) house

Read Chapters 5 and 6. There is one mistake in each sentence. Write the correct sentences.

1 The first PC, made in 1957, was large and cheap.
2 In 1976, Steve Jobs and Steve Wozniak started the Orange Computer Company.
3 Computer chips are getting smaller and slower every year.
4 Bill Gates was one of the first people to see the future of the TV.
5 Bill Gates began to study computer programming when he was eighteen.
6 The Windows operating system is more difficult to use than MS-DOS.

Read Chapter 7. Are these sentences true (T) or false (F)?

1 Microsoft built a computer called Deep Blue.
2 In 1997, Deep Blue beat the world's best chess player.
3 Computers are good at chess because it is a mathematical game.
4 Bill Gates invented a test to find out if a computer can think like a human.
5 A student won the Loebner Prize when he built a computer that could think.

Read Chapters 8 and 9. Fill in the gaps with these words.

advertise, blogs, eBay, free, Google MySpace, Napster, pixel, search, Wikipedia

1 A program that helps you to find information on the Web is called a _____ engine. The best known is _____, which is used a billion times a day.
2 You can buy or sell almost anything on the _____ website.

3 Companies who wanted to _____ on the Million Dollar Homepage paid one dollar for each _____.
4 When _____ first started, people could visit it to get free music.
5 The singer Lily Allen put her songs on _____, and thousands of people listened to them. A lot of people write _____ on this website, telling everyone what they are doing.
6 There is information about more than 6 million subjects on the _____ website, and it is all _____.

Read Chapter 10. Put these sentences in the correct order.

1 A lot of people began to buy PCs.
2 Samuel Morse invented a special code for messages.
3 People started to send text messages on their mobile phones.
4 The first telegraph machine was built.
5 People started to send e-mails using the Internet.
6 The telex machine was invented.

Read Chapter 11, then match these halves of sentences.

1 The first mobile phones were very heavy and expensive, . . .
2 It's difficult to write long text messages, . . .
3 Farmers in Bangladesh use mobile phones . . .
4 Every time someone makes a call on a mobile phone . . .
5 Mobile phones can make the roads more dangerous . . .
6 By the year 2015, there will probably be . . .

a the phone company keeps information about the call.
b about 4 billion mobile phone users in the world.
c but they were popular with rich young business people.
d because some people use them while they are driving.
e to find the best price for their food.
f so people use letters and numbers to make them shorter.

Read Chapter 12, then circle the correct words.

1 *Spacewar* was a computer game with *fast action* / *an interesting story*.

2 Nolan Bushnell started a company called *Atari* / *Sony*. He made a lot of money from a game called *Adventure* / *Pong*.

3 Nintendo make a games machine called *Wii* / *Xbox*.

4 People spend 20 *million* / *billion* dollars a year on computer games.

5 The game *Manhunt* was very *violent* / *funny*.

6 In 2005, a South Korean man *fell asleep* / *died* after playing a computer game for forty-nine hours.

Read Chapters 13 and 14. Choose the best question-word for these questions, and then answer them.

Why / *When* / *How* / *Where* / *What*

1 . . . was the first computer virus called?

2 . . . did the Jerusalem virus start to work?

3 . . . does the 'Dark Avenger' probably live?

4 . . . did the Melissa virus move from computer to computer?

5 . . . didn't the writer of the Sasser computer virus go to prison?

6 . . . was Abraham Abdallah's job?

7 . . . much money did Abdallah steal?

8 . . . did Philip Shortman have to go to prison?

Chapter 15 is called *The future*. Before you read it, can you guess what it is going to say? Circle Y (Yes) or N (No).

1 Soon we will probably be able to talk to computers. Y / N

2 Perhaps computers will be able to drive taxis. Y / N

3 PCs will continue to get smaller and smaller. Y / N

ACTIVITIES

After Reading

1 Use the clues to complete the puzzle.

1 Numbers and letters that contain a secret message (for example, 'Enigma' or 'Fish'). (4)

2 Part of a computer (or brain) that remembers information. (6)

3 A small, light computer that you can carry with you. (6)

4 Things that happened in the past. (7)

5 Programs that computers can read (for example, to play games or do calculations). (8)

6 A program that damages computers. (5)

7 To become twice as big or twice as many. (6)

8 To let other people use something that is yours. (5)

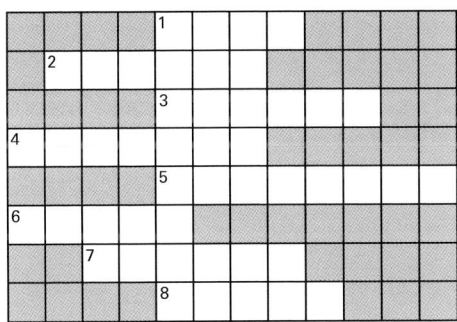

The hidden word is _____.

1 What was it?

2 When and where was it built?

3 How did it get its name?

4 What was it used for?

2 **Perhaps this is what some of the people in the book are thinking. Who are they, and what are they thinking about?**

1 'Mr Babbage is planning to build a new machine. He says it will even have a kind of memory, so it can do long, difficult calculations. But someone must write instructions for it – someone who understands the machine. I'm going to try!'

2 'This is crazy! I've been playing chess all my life, but IBM think their computer can beat me. It's only a machine. How can it understand chess? Oh no! It's going to win!'

3 'I'll never be able to buy a house. I don't have enough money, and I don't have anything valuable to sell. What if I trade something small for something a bit bigger? I can do it on the Internet. If I keep going, maybe I'll get a house in the end!'

4 'Engineers have to spend a lot of time doing difficult calculations. I'm going to invent a machine that will help. It will do the calculations for them!'

5 'Lots of people have computers now. But they're still difficult to use – you have to give the computer instructions using special words. I'm going to write software that lets people work their computers using pictures, not words. '

6 'These secret messages are important. But they're in code. If we can understand the code, we can find out what the Germans are planning to do. It will help us win the war!'

3 **How do you feel about computers and information technology? Complete some of these sentences.**

1 For me, the *best / worst* thing about computers is _____.

2 I *like / prefer not* to use a computer when _____.

3 The *best / worst* thing about mobile phones is _____.

4 I think that buying things on the Internet is a *good / bad* idea because _____.

5 I think that learning how to use information technology *is / is not* important because _____.

4 **Talk to an older person about information technology and how life has changed since they were young. Then write some sentences in a table like this.**

NOW	IN THE PAST
We can watch cinema anytime on DVD.	They watched TV and went to the cinema, but they didn't have DVDs.

Ask about some of these subjects:

− using computers, calculators, and other information technology at school

− listening to music and playing games

− using the telephone, and sending messages and e-mails to friends

5 **Find out more about robots. If you can, print some pictures of robots and write about them. The website www.wikipedia.org can help you: try searching for 'Robot', 'ASIMO', 'Roboraptor', 'Robosapien', and 'Aibo'.**

ABOUT THE AUTHOR

Paul A. Davies was born in Croydon, near London, and went to school there, but moved away as soon as possible. After leaving school, he spent a year in Reus, a town in Catalonia in northern Spain, teaching English by day and playing trumpet and piano in a band by night. He returned, reluctantly, to study English and Modern Languages at Oxford University. The highlight of his three-year course was a three-week trip to Edinburgh, where he and some fellow students staged an original musical at the annual Fringe Festival.

After working as an editor with Oxford University Press for five years, Paul left in 1998 to become a writer. Since then, he has written primary and secondary courses for many different ELT markets, as well as videos, readers, and multimedia material. He currently lives in Oxford with his wife and two young children. If he had any spare time, he would enjoy playing tennis, going to the gym, and playing music.

Paul has a love-hate relationship with information technology: he loves exploring the range of new possibilities which computers and other technological gadgets open up, but hates the fact that they never work properly. Nevertheless, he upgrades his mobile phone at every opportunity and has recently joined the MySpace generation by creating a homepage which, so far, has received no visitors at all.

OXFORD BOOKWORMS LIBRARY

Classics • Crime & Mystery • Factfiles • Fantasy & Horror
Human Interest • Playscripts • Thriller & Adventure
True Stories • World Stories

The OXFORD BOOKWORMS LIBRARY provides enjoyable reading in English, with a wide range of classic and modern fiction, non-fiction, and plays. It includes original and adapted texts in seven carefully graded language stages, which take learners from beginner to advanced level. An overview is given on the next pages.

All Stage 1 titles are available as audio recordings, as well as over eighty other titles from Starter to Stage 6. All Starters and many titles at Stages 1 to 4 are specially recommended for younger learners. Every Bookworm is illustrated, and Starters and Factfiles have full-colour illustrations.

The OXFORD BOOKWORMS LIBRARY also offers extensive support. Each book contains an introduction to the story, notes about the author, a glossary, and activities. Additional resources include tests and worksheets, and answers for these and for the activities in the books. There is advice on running a class library, using audio recordings, and the many ways of using Oxford Bookworms in reading programmes. Resource materials are available on the website <www.oup.com/elt/bookworms>.

The *Oxford Bookworms Collection* is a series for advanced learners. It consists of volumes of short stories by well-known authors, both classic and modern. Texts are not abridged or adapted in any way, but carefully selected to be accessible to the advanced student.

You can find details and a full list of titles in the *Oxford Bookworms Library Catalogue* and *Oxford English Language Teaching Catalogues*, and on the website <www.oup.com/elt/bookworms>.

THE OXFORD BOOKWORMS LIBRARY
GRADING AND SAMPLE EXTRACTS

STARTER • 250 HEADWORDS

present simple – present continuous – imperative –
can/*cannot, must* – *going to* (future) – simple gerunds …

Her phone is ringing – but where is it?

Sally gets out of bed and looks in her bag. No phone.
She looks under the bed. No phone. Then she looks behind
the door. There is her phone. Sally picks up her phone and
answers it. *Sally's Phone*

STAGE 1 • 400 HEADWORDS

… past simple – coordination with *and*, *but*, *or* –
subordination with *before, after, when, because, so* …

I knew him in Persia. He was a famous builder and I
worked with him there. For a time I was his friend, but
not for long. When he came to Paris, I came after him –
I wanted to watch him. He was a very clever, very dangerous
man. *The Phantom of the Opera*

STAGE 2 • 700 HEADWORDS

… present perfect – *will* (future) – *(don't) have to, must not, could* –
comparison of adjectives – simple *if* clauses – past continuous –
tag questions – *ask*/*tell* + infinitive …

While I was writing these words in my diary, I decided
what to do. I must try to escape. I shall try to get down the
wall outside. The window is high above the ground, but
I have to try. I shall take some of the gold with me – if I
escape, perhaps it will be helpful later. *Dracula*

STAGE 3 • 1000 HEADWORDS

... should, may – present perfect continuous – *used to* – past perfect
– causative – relative clauses – indirect statements ...

Of course, it was most important that no one should see Colin, Mary, or Dickon entering the secret garden. So Colin gave orders to the gardeners that they must all keep away from that part of the garden in future. ***The Secret Garden***

STAGE 4 • 1400 HEADWORDS

... past perfect continuous – passive (simple forms) –
would conditional clauses – indirect questions –
relatives with *where/when* – gerunds after prepositions/phrases ...

I was glad. Now Hyde could not show his face to the world again. If he did, every honest man in London would be proud to report him to the police. ***Dr Jekyll and Mr Hyde***

STAGE 5 • 1800 HEADWORDS

... future continuous – future perfect –
passive (modals, continuous forms) –
would have conditional clauses – modals + perfect infinitive ...

If he had spoken Estella's name, I would have hit him. I was so angry with him, and so depressed about my future, that I could not eat the breakfast. Instead I went straight to the old house. ***Great Expectations***

STAGE 6 • 2500 HEADWORDS

... passive (infinitives, gerunds) – advanced modal meanings –
clauses of concession, condition

When I stepped up to the piano, I was confident. It was as if I knew that the prodigy side of me really did exist. And when I started to play, I was so caught up in how lovely I looked that I didn't worry how I would sound. ***The Joy Luck Club***

BOOKWORMS · FACTFILES · STAGE 3

Recycling

SUE STEWART

What will we do when there is nowhere to put our rubbish? Every day, all over the world, people drop cans, boxes, paper, and bottles into bins and never think about them again. And the rubbish mountains get bigger and bigger.

But there is another way – a way that makes old paper into houses, broken bottles into jewellery, and old cans into bridges. Anyone can recycle – it's easy, it saves money, and it's a way to say, 'I care about the Earth.' Saving the world starts with you – here and now.

BOOKWORMS · FACTFILES · STAGE 3

Martin Luther King

ALAN C. McLEAN

The United States in the 1950s and 60s was a troubled place. Black people were angry, because they did not have the same rights as whites. It was a time of angry words, of marches, of protests, a time of bombs and killings.

But above the angry noise came the voice of one man – a man of peace. 'I have a dream,' said Martin Luther King, and it was a dream of blacks and whites living together in peace and freedom. This is the story of an extraordinary man, who changed American history in his short life.